PAR~~ENTS STOP~~:

DON'T GIVE UP,

THERE IS HOPE!

By Elizabeth W. Brown

Parents Stop! Don't Give Up, There Is Hope!
by Elizabeth W. Brown

ISBN # 0-89228-116-2

Copyright ©, 1996
  Elizabeth W. Brown

Published for the author by
  Impact Christian Books, Inc.
  332 Leffingwell, Suite 101,
  Kirkwood, Mo. 63122

Printed in the United States of America

DEDICATION

This book is dedicated to you, parents, for your hard work in nurturing your children in the way of the Lord. May you be strengthened and encouraged and blessed as you read this book. Your labor is not in vain.

I also dedicate this book to my loving husband for his support and help, and to my children for their patience and understanding as I took time to complete this book.

My thanks to my parents who have always been there for me with their kind, supportive and encouraging words. A special thanks to my father who has been a motivating factor in my life by his constant reminder to his children that knowledge is a major key to success and how much we need it.

My thanks to all my friends for their prayers, and to a special friend for giving of her valuable time in helping to proofread, edit and modify this book.

My thanks to the editors for making this book pleasant and attractive reading material for the reader.

May God richly bless you all.

CONTENTS

*LO, CHILDREN ARE AN HERITAGE OF THE LORD:
AND THE FRUIT OF THE WOMB ARE HIS REWARD.*
(PSALM 127:3)

*CHILDREN'S CHILDREN ARE THE CROWN OF OLD
MEN; AND THE GLORY OF CHILDREN ARE THEIR
FATHERS.*
(PROVERBS 17:6)

INTRODUCTION

Are you discouraged about the direction in which your child is heading?

Are you troubled about your child's future?

Are you concerned that your child is not interested in the things of God?

Are you about to give up on your child, or have you already given up?

Does it seem like there is no hope for your child?

It is not a coincidence that you picked up this book to read.

God wants to speak to you today, He has a word for you.

About three years ago the Lord spoke to my heart to write this book as an encouragement to parents who were on the brink of giving up hope in their children. If you are discouraged about the direction in which your child is heading and you feel powerless trying to help change the course of that direction, if you have been searching for answers regarding problems you are encountering with your child, this book is for you.

As the parent of a teenage daughter, I can relate to parents who are battling with questions regarding their children's behavior and can't seem to get answers. I, too, was once in the same predicament. But after searching intensely for answers regarding my daughter's behavior and having no success, I turned to God's Word for help. God in his infinite wisdom, and grace, enlightened my understanding to His position, as well as to my own position in the matter. Because of this enlightenment, I now have peace and better understanding to deal with my daughter's behavior.

I am convinced that after reading this book, you too will experience that same peace and confidence that I am experiencing.

Chapter 1

GOD'S ORIGINAL PLAN INCLUDED YOUR CHILD

God Almighty, who established His Word before the foundation of the world, wants you to know this day that when He inspired holy men to write the Scriptures, He had you in mind. You, your family, and all that pertains to you, were His priority. God had your child's welfare in mind, and therefore made provisions in His Word to cover every aspect of what would confront either you or your child. Your child is an integral part of God's plan for promoting His kingdom's business.

He wants you to know that He has your child's best interests in mind. He desires to see your child succeed in every aspect of his life. He desires to see that your child rises to the heights of his potential. God wants to see your child in good health. He wants to see your child live life to its fullest. Most of all, He wants to see your child saved!

God has a tremendous plan for your child. Read and see the good things God planned for your child. He has good things in store for him.

I will be discussing some promises that God made to you and to your child in this book. As you read through them, you will be encouraged and your confidence will be built up.

Currently, you may be facing some very difficult times with your child. You may have tried all you could and nothing you have done seems to have worked. You may have wondered "Where is God, why hasn't He intervened?"

God's Word will answer your questions. Hebrew 13:5 says that God promised never to leave you neither would He forsake you.

So where is God? He is right there with you in the midst of all you are going through, working all things together to bring out the very best for you. This is God's Word and He means what He says. It is important that you, as parents, know and believe without any doubt that the God who loves you with an everlasting love promised never to leave you nor to forsake you. He also told you in Jeremiah 33:3, "Call unto me, and I will answer thee, and shew thee great and mighty things, which thou knowest not." It really does not matter how grave the situation may look, God promised that if you call upon Him, He will answer you and show you great and mighty things that you had no idea He would do.

The enemy wants you to question God when things are not working out like you expect. But I Corinthians 13:12 tells you that you look through the glass darkly, meaning the full measure or the full picture of all that is taking place around you is obscured. Your natural eyes cannot see things that are happening in the spirit realm. This is why you have to rely on the God who sees all things and knows all things.

Nothing is hidden from His sight. You have to rely on Him totally. He is God Omniscient - All Knowing.

"Know unto God are all His works from the beginning of the world." (Acts 15:18)

"Neither is there any creature that is not manifested in His sight: but all things are naked and opened unto the eyes of Him with whom we have to do." (Hebrews 4:13)

"But as it is written, Eye hath not seen, nor ear heard, neither have it entered into the heart of man, the things which God hath prepared for them that love Him.

But God hath revealed them unto us by His Spirit: for the Spirit searcheth all things, yea, the deep things of God.

For what man knoweth the things of a man, save the spirit of man which is in him?

Even so the things of God knoweth no man, but the Spirit of God."

(I Cor. 2:9-11)

God is aware of every thing that is happening in your life; in the spirit realm as well as the natural realm. Based on His supreme knowledge of this, He works everything out for your good. It is important that you know this and trust God.

You are living in a deceptive time, Satan is attacking in every way possible with the hope that he will cause you to give up and fall. If you are to survive his deception, you must believe God's Word to be true, and hold firmly to it no matter what comes up against you. If you don't, you leave yourself open for defeat.

There was a time in my life, when I was going through a severe crisis. I felt like I was all alone in my battle; I sometimes felt like God had left me. But I later discovered that was not true, God had not left me, the fact is, I left God. I gave up when things didn't go according to my expectations. I stopped believing God's promises. When I was going through the most difficult times, when I experienced my weakest moments, God was right there by my side manifesting His strength in my weakness or just pouring His strength into me during my weakest moments.

> *"And He said unto me, My grace is sufficient for thee: for my strength is made perfect in weakness...."*
>
> (II Corinthians 12:9b)

This is what God does for all His children. He never leaves them to walk alone. He stays with them in the heat of the battle, strengthening them every step of the way.

Aside from the power of God, you are no match for Satan. It is by the help of God, you have made it this far. Throughout your difficult times, God had been by your side, leading, guiding and directing you. God promised to be with you even to the end of the age. Nothing can stop that.

When you think that God has left you, most of the time, you have simply left Him. You are the one who stopped trusting Him. God wants you to be encouraged and to know that His promises are true. When He declares a thing, He will surely bring it to pass.

He tells you in Jeremiah 1:5,

> *"Before I formed thee in the belly I knew thee; and before thou camest forth out of the womb, I sanctified thee...."*

In order for you to benefit from this verse, you have to believe that God's Word applies to all of His children. All of His promises belong to you. You became an heir to God's promises through the shed blood of Jesus Christ.

> *"The Spirit itself beareth witness with our spirit, that we are the children of God. And if children, then heirs, heirs of God, and joint heirs with Christ...."*
>
> (Romans 8:16,17)

Jeremiah 1:5 applies to your child, if you can believe by faith. Mom, Dad, before you give up on your daughter or your son, look at this verse more carefully, and hear what the Lord is saying about your child.

According to Jeremiah 1:5, that daughter, that son, you have lost interest in, that child you are about to give up on, that child that everyone has lost hope in, that child that people say won't amount to anything, that child that has caused so much trouble, so much embarrassment to the family, is a special child. God is letting you know that your child is unique to Him. Your child is the finished product of His hands.

He has already completed His work in your child. While you are limited to seeing only the present state of your child, God sees the complete picture of your child's entire life.

What He sees is very good. God thinks good thoughts toward your child, and desires to give him a bright future. Look at your child through the eyes of God and see your child the way God sees him/her.

Let's go back to Jeremiah 1:5 and dissect the verse to establish a few important points.

First, the God who created the heavens and the earth, the God who created the mountains and the valleys formed your child. The God who created the world and all that is in it, formed your child. The God who created the entire universe in six days, looked over His creation and proclaimed that it was good, formed your child.

The God who never makes mistakes, formed your child. All that God made was very good, was complete, was perfect. God is complete in all of His doings. His standard is perfection. God made your child in His own image, not in anyone else's image, but in His OWN image. That is awesome! God wanted your child perfect, so He made him in His image. Therefore, your child is a child of perfection.

Before God even thought about forming your child in the womb, He already knew your child. The Hebrew word for know is *yada* which means "to understand in its entirety, to discern, to discover." Nothing about your child is a mystery to God. Before your child was formed, God perfectly understood his full potential.

He knew everything there was to know about your child. He knew the type of personality your child would have. He knew the types of behaviors your child would display. He knew what your child would look like, how your child would talk and how your child would act. Nothing is hidden from God. He was aware of what your child could handle and what he could not handle. Based on these factors and many others, God carefully and wonderfully put your child together.

> *"I will praise thee; for I am fearfully and wonderfully made; marvelous are thy works; and that my soul knoweth right well."* (Psalm 139:14)

Before forming your child, God also saw you and knew you. He saw your weaknesses and your strengths. He was confident that you were the right parent to whom He could entrust His precious one. Presently, you may be focusing on all the problems you are confronting in rearing your child. God built in you every mechanism you need to parent your child.

Even now, God is uniquely working everything together for the very good of both you and your child. God does not want you to look at the problems, instead, He wants you to look at what He can do. God does not make mistakes.

In spite of all the faults you see in your child, God is still able to make him His worthy heir.

God uses adversities to build up character in an individual. The adversities I encountered in my lifetime, helped to make me the person I am today. The Lord is building up my character. Your adversities helped to make you who you are today.

God is building character in your child with what He allows. God has purposes for whatever He allows your child to experience. Sometimes the situation may not appear good, but God will work it out in such a way that the outcome is molding material in him.

> *"And we know that all things work together*
> *for good to them that love God, to them who*
> *are called according to His purpose."*
> (Romans 8:28)

The Bible says "all things" not just some things, works for the good of those who love Him, who are called according to His purpose. All that God allows in your life leads to ultimate good.

Take an eleven-month-old boy who is walking, for example. He does not just get out of the crib one day and begin to walk the next day. The first time he tried to walk, he did not do so well, he fell lots of times, but that did not deter, discouraged, or stopped him from trying to walk. He tried again and again. Then one day, he didn't fall anymore. He stayed up. He had learned to walk. As he grew, he was able to walk firmly, confidently, and securely. This is how it is with some of our children. For some of them it will take much falling before they are able to stay up. They will make many mistakes before they get the message and eventually figure out what is right.

Satan also sets up road blocks on God's paths for your children's lives, hoping that those blockages will prevent them from accomplishing God's mighty plans for their lives. Your prayers are mighty weapons against Satan's work. It is also encouraging to know that those obstacles Satan sets up do not change God's plans for your child's life. God designed those road blocks so your child can learn, grow and overcome them. And He allows Satan to place them again and again until your child learns. The road blocks may cause what you think are setbacks, but God had already provided for them.

> Mark 11:24,   *"What things soever ye desire, when ye pray believe that ye receive them, and ye shall have them."*
>
> John 15:7,   *"If you abide in me, and my words abide in you, ye shall ask what ye will and it shall be done unto you."*
>
> I John 5:14,   *"And this is the confidence that we have in Him, that if we ask anything according to His will, He heareth us."*

There is a story about a woman of God named Hannah

in I Samuel Chapter one. Hannah prayed to God for a son. She desired that the child she asked God for would be a servant in the house of the Lord. God gave Hannah her heart's desire, she had a son. His name was Samuel. He grew up as a servant in the house of the Lord. Samuel became one of the greatest prophets and judges in the history of Israel. God will bring His Word to pass in your life if you can believe it to be true and to mean exactly what it says. God promised to you, if you abide in Him, that is, if you remain in Him, if you stand fast in Him, if you live by His requirements in His Word, do what He says do, if you keep your eyes on Him, He will do whatever you ask. You must ask in faith believing that He will do whatever you ask.

I John 5:14 says to be confident that if you ask anything according to His will, He will hear you. God does not desire that any man, including your child, die in his sins. Instead, He wants all men to turn away from their sins and follow Him.

> *"The Lord is not slack concerning His promise, as some men count slackness; but is longsuffering to us-ward, not willing that any should perish, but that all should come to repentance."* (II Peter 3:9)

This verse lets you know that when you pray and ask God to save your child, you are praying in accordance with the will of God, therefore, He will hear your prayers and answer you.

"...God is no respecter of persons."
(Acts 10:34b)

Just as He heard and answered Hannah's prayers, He will hear and answer your prayers when you pray in faith.

Be encouraged and know that God sees everything that is transpiring in your child's life. He has not forgotten about you or your child, neither has He forgotten about His promises to you concerning your child. However, He does have a time for everything. As Solomon said in Ecclesiastes 3:1, *"To every thing there is a season, and a time to every purpose under the heaven."*

The Master-Builder, who is our Lord Jesus Christ, is at work in your child's life, using adversities your child encountered to build the right character that will make him God's unique servant. He is forming, molding and perfecting your child. He is fine-tuning your child, putting His finishing touches on him, when He gets through, your child will come out as fine gold. Allow His time to take its course. God has not given up on your child, neither should you give up on your child. Hold on to God's Word and trust Him as He works in the life of your child. God has not completed His work in your child yet.

In the beginning, when God was creating the things of the world, He didn't announce that His work was good in the beginning stages of His creations. He only announced *"it is good"* (Genesis 1:10) when He completed a specific task. God does not focus on the infancy stage of His work. His concern is with the finished product. The final product is what matters.

The process involved in making the product is not the question here. How the product comes out in the end, is what matters. And for your peace of mind, God never made any thing over. It didn't matter what the content of the thing was, when He touched it, it came out good. God specializes in making great things out of nothing.

How does God see your child? He sees your child as he will eventually turn out.

He sees your child as being sanctified, consecrated, separated from an earthly use!

He sees your child set aside purposely for His service.

How about you? How do you see your child?

Chapter 2

DOING IT GOD'S WAY

I became very frustrated whenever I saw my child going against the teachings of God. I was inexperienced in how to properly reach her. I screamed and fussed at her, hoping to force her back into the way of the Lord. Things got worse.

I did not look to see what made her act the way she did. I sometimes operated with a one track mind. I had a preconceived notion of how she should behave. And when her actions did not match up to my expectations, I sometimes went off on her, which did not help the situation. I eventually realized that I was getting nowhere by fussing and screaming, that it did not solve the problem.

The more I fussed, the more she would put up a wall between us, and I could not get through to her. I needed to seek God's wisdom on how to reach my daughter. I needed to seek God's guidance in the matter. I had to remember that I could not change my child. I had no power to draw her to God.

The best thing I could have done for my daughter was

to be Christlike before her. I was to show her love and treat her with kindness. I was to continue to reveal the Word of God to her. This is part of my responsibility as a parent.

> *"Therefore shall you lay up these my words in your heart and in your soul, and bind them for a sign upon your hand, that they may be as frontlet between your eyes.*
>
> *And ye shall teach them your children, speaking of them when thou sittest in thine house, and when thou walkest by the way, when thou liest down, and when thou risest up."* (Deut. 11:18-19)

This passage applies to all believing parents. Not only does God command you to bind His Word upon your hand and place them between your eyes and in constant view, He commands you to teach your child His Word at all times of the day. You cannot give the excuse that you are too busy and do not have the time to teach your child the Word of God. There is no compromise with this command.

God requires that you be His teacher to your child. He entrusted His precious one to you and relies on you to teach him His Word. It is not the Sunday School teacher's responsibility to assure that your child learns the Word of God. God did not give that responsibility to him. God gave it to you.

I learned this lesson when my daughter was almost seven years old. I thought it was enough to take her to Sunday School. I didn't realize the urgency of embedding the Word in her at an early age and also of modeling the Word before her.

When I finally realized that I had not been responsible in that area, I tried to play catch-up and overwhelmed her with the Word. She became resentful of that and I became frustrated, simply because my approach was wrong. What I should have done was to prayerfully approach the task, develop a teaching method that was geared toward her learning pace, and then lovingly and carefully teach her the Word. In God's mercy, He gradually began to show me how to teach my child His Word appropriately.

You may wonder when is the best time to start instructing a child in the Word of God. I would say, start before he is born. Get him accustomed to hearing the Word. I have heard of parents who read to their children while the children were still in the womb, and that's an excellent beginning. This puts the parent in the habit of reading to the child. I do not mean to bring guilt on any parent who did not start teaching his child the Word at an early age. If you missed that chance, it is still not too late. You can begin today.

Proverb 22:6 says, *"Train up a child in the way he should go: and when he is old, he will not depart from it."*

The Hebrew word for train is *"chanak,"* which means "primary" or "root." It also means "to initiate or discipline." "To train" indicates the first instruction that a child receives.

I believe the first instruction a child receives should be

from the Word of God. Teach him the difference between right and wrong based on God's Word. Two things that should be a daily part of any Christian home are prayer and the study of God's Word. It is essential that parents make time for daily devotion in their home.

God established certain standards and principles for man to live by. He expects parents to instruct their children in those principles. It should also be remembered that teaching the Word, must also be followed by example in order for it to be effective. If you expect your child to pray and read the Word, you too must pray and read the Word. If you expect your child to be kind, you too must model kindness. If you want him to be friendly, you too must be friendly. If you want him to be respectful, be respectful to others. If you want him to love others, you too must show love. You are representing God before your child.

Part of this training also has to do with correcting wrong behaviors at an early age. Some parents may think nothing of a young child talking back, hitting them, or saying a few wrong words to them. What they fail to realize is, if these negative behaviors are not corrected at an early age, they will be carried into adolescence. If you don't want your child talking back to you when he is old, stop him from backing-talking while he is young. Whatever you allow now, expect later. Mold and shape your child now while he is young and manageable, and when he is old, he won't depart from it. As someone put it, "If you bend them now, you won't have to break them later."

A wise parent will begin disciplinary actions early to prevent future embarrassment. Believe me, I am speaking from experience.

Another part of this training should be designed to expose the child to the manner of life for which he is intended. Commence the child's education in the way he is bent. This is of great importance to the child.

Start by observing your child. Find out what activities your child enjoys doing best and gear his education toward those activities. For example, if your child likes to write, get him English lessons. If he likes to sing, get him music lessons. If he likes to swim, get him swimming lessons. If he likes to draw, get him into art lessons.

I later learned that one of the causes of my daughter's behavior problem was boredom. The child had nothing to do during her spare time. She was bored. I never really took the time to find out what she enjoyed doing. I was too busy with work and everything else. When I did try to get her involved in extra curriculum activities, I put her in the wrong class. I remember at one point putting her into piano lessons because I had always admired people who played the piano, and thought that would be a good activity for her.

Notice I said, what *I thought*, not what she could be good at. Well, she didn't like the class and did not do well. That was not her interest. So I took her out of the class but never bothered to find out what she enjoyed doing. So she spent most of her idle time getting into trouble. As someone has put it, "An idle mind is the devil's work bench." I recognized my mistake almost too late.

Please do not make the same mistake I made. Take notice of your children, find out what interests them, not what interests you. Then gear their education toward those interests.

While we are on the subject of training up children by God's method, let us focus our attention on some instructions given by Solomon, the wisest man in biblical times.

"Withhold not correction from thy child; For if thou beat him with the rod, he will not die, Thou shalt beat him with the rod, and shalt deliver his soul from hell."
(Proverbs 23:13)

"He that spareth his rod hateth his son; But he that loveth him chasteneth him betimes."
(Proverbs 13:24)

"Correct thy son and he will give thee rest; Yes, he will give delight unto thy soul."
(Proverbs 29:17)

"The rod and reproof give wisdom: but a child left to himself bringeth his mother shame."
(Proverbs 29:15)

I have heard some parents say, "Oh I just hate to spank my child, it just hurts me." These parents may think they love their children, but according to Scripture, those parents actually hate their children, in the sense that they are setting their children up for the judicial system to enforce a much

28

tougher disciplinary action on them later. The Bible tells us in Proverbs 13:24, *"He that spares the rod hates his child."* When the rod is used for correction, it demonstrates a parent's love for his child and implies that the parent desires to save the child from future destruction and embarrassment. Hebrews 12:6 tells us that, *"For whom the Lord loveth, He chasteneth...."* Jesus disciplines those He loves. When a parent loves his child, he disciplines him.

The rod used as a form of disciplinary action, not only benefits the child, it also protects the parents from future shame.

When a parent fails to discipline his child, he puts the child at a disadvantage when he later faces the real world and discovers how things are really supposed to be. God gave parents the duty of nurturing their children in His Word. This nurturing causes the children to grow spiritually.

In the society in which we live, it can be said that the parent is failing in his Christian duty. In the society in which we live, if a parent neglects his duty, the judicial system won't. The wisdom of God is to use the rod of correction now and deliver your child from hell later. Proper nourishment is twofold. One discourages evil behavior by way of punishment and the other encourages right doings by way of the Word and example.

I understand that using the rod for correction has become a very controversial subject, however, this is the method provided by God, and it has proven to be a success. Great men and women can and have attested to this fact.

The rod when used properly and correctly will never harm a child, instead, it will make him a better person, and one day he will thank you for using it.

The rod should never be used in harshness, anger, retaliation or as an abusive tool. It should be used in love, and with understanding. Apply it only when the need demands, and just enough to get results without being abusive to the child.

Always show affection to your child by your kind words and support. They will give him the assurance and confidence needed to help him develop emotionally. By doing so you provide him with an atmosphere, in which he feels secure and loved, and it becomes easier for him to talk to you when he has a personal problem and needs someone to talk to or needs a shoulder to cry on. Believe me, I am writing from my own experience through trial and error. It is vital to establish a good relationship with your child while he is still young. Don't let that chance pass you by.

Be careful not to demonstrate partiality among your children. Children can sense differences and can easily feel left out. In all you do, be fair. Provide a caring and loving atmosphere in your home. Give your children plenty of love and shower them with lots of hugs, but keep the rules the same for all.

By all means follow through on your promises to your children. Some parents have a tendency to make promises to their children, getting their hopes up, and then do not follow through. This discourages children, especially if they were really looking forward to the thing promised.

When you make a promise to your child, he counts on you to keep your promise. He may have spent all weekend thinking about what had been promised and looking forward to receiving what you promised. If it doesn't happen, it's a big let down for him.

You have to remember that children are people, too; they have feelings. They don't like being let down any more than you do as an adult.

I once asked my younger daughter how she felt when I didn't follow through on promises that I had made to her. She said, "Not too good, just like today when you promised to buy me a sleeping bag; I was excited all day at school. I was looking forward to going to buy it after school. I could hardly wait for school to let out, so we could go. But when you told me that you couldn't take me to get it, I felt really bad."

I noticed the sad look on her face as she expressed her feelings, and I couldn't help but take her. I really didn't have anything pressing, I was just tired and didn't feel like driving. I had not realized that postponing the shopping would bother her so much.

We parents have a tendency to consider some things as insignificant, that our children consider very important. I admit I have been guilty in this area, but after communicating with my children I am learning not to make promises I cannot keep. I try my best to keep every promise, but if I don't, they will not let me forget it. They usually say, "But, Mamie, you said!" They believe what I say and expect me to carry it through.

Parents, your children believe what *you* say and expect you to make your word good. So try in every way possible to keep your promises to them. I do understand that you may not always be able to keep every promise, but even in those cases, explain to them why you could not follow through. Tell them that you are sorry, and try to make it up by doing something special with, or for, them. You may want to ask them how you can make it up to them.

Listen to your children. If you don't, they may go out and find someone (a person who may not be someone you approve of) who will take the time to listen. Talk with your children, encourage them and spend quality time with them. Do things with them that interest them. Be a friend to your children. Sacrifice your time now for a lifetime of fulfillment.

Chapter 3

LEARNING TO SURRENDER TO GOD

After you have done your best to rear your child in a godly manner, teaching him the things of the Lord, investing your time, energy and resources in the development of his life, then one day you wake up to find that your child has chosen a way contrary to the way of God. What do you do? This is the question millions of parents are asking. They find it difficult to deal with this change. In my experience, I find that the best way to handle a situation like this, is to surrender the child over to God. This is not the time to fight, this not the time to argue, this is not the time to hold on to your child. This is not the time to regret, wishing you could have done it differently. This is the time to pray, trust God, and surrender your child over to God.

You have done your part, the rest is in God's hand. You made have not been the perfect parent, but in most cases, you probably did what you knew was best at the time to be a good parent in leading your child in the right way.

At this point, you can do nothing in your own power to change your child's mind. But there is One who can, and that One is none other but our Lord and Savior Jesus Christ. He can do the impossible. He is your source of help. As you begin to pray fervently in faith on behalf of your child, our God who is sovereign will hear your prayers and answer you.

Remember the words of James, *"...The effectual prayer of a righteous man availeth much."* (James 5:16b) Your diligent and earnest prayer carries with it a tremendous amount of power and it can change the course of things.

I am reminded of the prodigal son in Luke 15:12-32. This son had the best that life had to offer. His father provided all he could ever need, yet the son was not satisfy. He thought there was something out there he was missing in his life. So he decided to go out and see. One day he asked his father for his portion of the inheritance. He was leaving for what he thought was a better lifestyle. His father did not question his son's request, did not argue with him, did not try to hold him back, instead, he gave the boy his portion of the inheritance and the boy left to experience what life was all about out there.

Some would look at the father's reaction to the boy's request and think that the father didn't care or didn't love his son. But I believe this father cared and loved his son dearly. I believe the father tried in his own way to assure that his son had the best of things, he seemed to be a very generous man. All of that did not make the boy content. He chose to go contrary to the way of his father. His father knew his son was making a wrong choice. He knew life could be tough out there. Everything was not as glamorous as his son imagined it to be. There was also hatred, greed, selfishness, and many other evil behaviors out there that his son could not comprehend at the time. This father probably understood his son well enough to know that nothing he could have said would have changed the boy's mind from leaving. The son wanted his freedom, he wanted out and that's all that mattered to him at the time. So his father gave the boy the opportunity to do just that even if it meant suffering in the process. The father realized that there comes a time in one's life when he must gain his own experience and find things out on his own. This sounds tough, but it is true love. This could also be viewed as a form of chastening to the son he loved, to turn him back on the right track.

I believe all along, the father had a notion or expected that his son would return once he came face to face with the evil out there and realized his mistakes. As the story goes, life began to take its toll on the son. He foolishly lavished all of his inheritance, and descended as low as eating with pigs in the pig pen. When he came to his senses and realized that what his father had was far better than what was out there, the son eventually returned home to his father, and felt remorse for what he had done.

This is a tough lesson, but some children only learn the hard way. I understand it is not easy to release your precious ones, especially when you know they have chosen a way that will cause them pain and suffering. Sometimes, experience is the only teacher from whom they can learn. In spite of which direction your child chooses, always model the love of Christ before him.

Remember you represent Christ. You are to show His love to your child. You are to love him in spite of his actions. Love him just the way he is. If this is difficult for you to do, pray and ask God to help you in that area, He will give you the strength to do just that. It is love that will draw your child to the Lord. God does not stop loving us because we disobey Him. He continues to love us although He hates disobedience. God said, *"Yet I love thee with an everlasting love: therefore with loving kindness have I drawn thee"* (Jeremiah 31:3) His love for us never ceases.

You are to show the same love toward your child. You can not stop loving him because he trays away from God's way. You have to love him the way God loves him.

God loves him with an unconditional, never ending love. In other words, you are to love your child unconditionally, love him regardless of his behavior. You do not like what he does but you love him as your child.

As you continue to pray for your child, God will fulfill His promise to you. He will allow circumstances to come your child's way, that will cause him to recognize Christ in his life. And by His grace your child will give his life to the Lord. Trust God, no matter what condition your child is in, God is in control. According to Luke 1:37, *"Nothing is impossible with God."* Believe me, God has a lesson in every adversity your child faces. He has a good purpose for allowing it.

Sometimes people have a preconceived notion of how

God should operate and when He should move. When God does not move according to their time table, they get impatient, sometimes even get angry with God give up on God. Consequently, losing the opportunity to see God work out the situation.

Don't make that mistake. Know that you serve a loving God who has your best interest, your growth and development in mind. He is God. He is in control of all things. He is the One who has His plans for your life, therefore, leads you accordingly. When you pray in faith and ask God to move in a certain situation for you, know that whatever time He chooses to do it, is the right time.

God does not think like people think. He does not move on man's time table. No one has the ability to figure God out. He made this perfectly clear in Isaiah 55:7-9:

> *"Let the wicked forsake his way, and the unrighteous man his thoughts..., For my thoughts are not your thoughts, neither are my ways your ways, saith the Lord. For as the heavens are higher than the earth, so are my ways higher than your ways, and my thoughts than your thoughts."*

Again, God does not think like man thinks, and therefore, He can never operate on man's thought patterns. But rest assure that His timing is perfect.

It may appear that God is taking too long to save your child, but be encouraged and know that God is not slow as man may think. It is God's desire that your child come to know Him.

God said, "Be careful for nothing, but in everything by prayer and thanksgiving let your request be made known unto God." (Philippians 4:6) Instead of being anxious, God wants you to pray and make your request known to Him. He wants you to trust Him and give Him thanks because He is working everything out in your best interest. I believe that God sometimes allows His people to experience certain situations to teach them patience. There are those who lack the attribute of patience. I believe God allows them to get into situations where they can learn how to exercise patience.

When you have experienced the goodness of the Lord in times past, when you know Him to be true, when you know, and know the God you serve, know how He has come through for you in the pass, and you deliberately give up on your God because He is not moving according to your plans, do you know what you are, in essence, implying? You are saying, "Lord, your Word is not true, I do not believe it."

Sometimes Christians who have been with the Lord for a substantial amount of time can sometimes act like babes in the Lord. They still feed on milk when they should be feeding on meat. As Paul told the Corinthians,

> *"I feed you with milk and not with meat for hitherto you were not able to bear it, neither yet now are ye able."*
>
> (I Corinthians 3:2)

When Paul first led the Corinthians to the Lord, they were babes in the Lord, they did not know the ways of God, so he had to instruct them on their level of comprehension at the time, he understood that they could not handle the meat of the Word at the time. Now that they had been with the Lord for a period of time, Paul expected more from them. He expected them to have grown and to have matured spiritually. Just as we advance from one level to the next in school so should our spiritual growth in the Lord. We grow from level to level, from height to height.

A baby Christian lacks the knowledge in the Word and is inexperienced in the ways of God. It is really not too surprising when he demonstrates lack of patience when it comes to waiting for the move of God in a certain situation. However, it is another story when it comes to a mature Christian, someone who has been with the Lord for a substantial amount of time. The mature Christian believes God's Word: He knows and understands that God desires the best for him and his child. He knows the power of prayer. For these reasons he is able to exercise faith in God, knowing that no matter how long it takes God to move in a certain situation, the ultimate end will be good.

Chapter 4

HOW SHOULD YOU PRAY
FOR YOUR CHILD

When your pray for your child, start calling those things that be not as though they were. (Romans 4:17)

Be an example of God our father, he called Abraham the father of many nations even before Abraham was ever a father. (Genesis 17:4).

You have to believe and pray the Word of God for your child. When you pray in faith desiring the same things that God desires for your child, you can be assured that your prayers are being answered.

It's time to start praying a "prayer of faith", such as: *Father, I thank You for giving me a godly child, I thank you, for You knew my child before he was conceived, You formed my child, You established his path, You know his way. Lord I thank you for giving me a holy child. I thank you for giving me a righteous child. Father, You have set my child apart for Your service, I thank you. Lord, I thank You for before I gave birth to my child you had already sanctified him. Lord, you said that the fruit of my womb is blessed, I thank You that my child is blessed.*

Lord, according to Your Word, if I train up my child in the way he should go, my child will not depart from that way. Father, I thank You that my child will not depart from your way. Lord, I thank you for giving my child your peace. You said in Your Word that my child will be taught of the Lord and great shall be his peace. Father, I thank you, for your Word is true, and You watch over your Word to perform it. I know Lord, You are bringing your Word to pass in my child's life.

Believe God even as Abraham did. When God promised him a son, he believed God. (Genesis 15:1-6) Although Abraham was almost one hundred years old, the Bible says he did not consider His own dead body, neither did he consider the deadness of Sarah's (his wife's) womb. But he was strong in the faith and was fully persuaded that what God has promised in His Word, He is well able to perform. (Romans 4:18-21) Surely, God will perform His Word.

Nothing is too hard for God to do. You can even remind God of His promises. It is not wrong to do so. In Isaiah 43:26, God said bring to His remembrance those things He had promised.

Parent, if you will start praying the Word of God over your child, calling those things that are not as though they were, you will see your child in a whole new prospective. You will experience the peace of knowing that your child is assured a bright future.

"Then saith He unto His disciples, the harvest truly is plenteous, but the laborers are few; pray ye therefore the Lord of the harvest, that He will send forth laborers into His harvest." (Matthew 9:37-38)

Just as Jesus told His disciples to pray that the Lord will send laborers into His harvest. He wants you also to pray so the Lord of the harvest can send laborers to your child with the gospel message. If you have a child who is not saved, that child is still part of God's harvest field. He wants him to come and be part of His kingdom. Pray that your child will be uncomfortable in the world of sin. Pray that God's angel will arrest him and make his heart ready to receive His word.

If you cannot reach your child with the gospel message, God has someone out there who can reach him. As you pray in faith, God will send a laborer who will reach your child with the Good News of Jesus Christ. The enemy knows the power of prayer and he is also aware of God's promises for your child. He does not want you claiming those promises for your child and does not want you praying for them. That is why he tries his very best to distract you from praying. He tries to keep you in an angry, sad, and depressed state of mind. He keeps you anxious and worried about your child, which actually shows lack of faith in God. All of these are schemes Satan uses to prevent you from focusing on God's promises and blessings for you and your child.

I remember when I first noticed a change in my daughter's behavior. I could see that she was going contrary to the teachings of God, going astray from the godly teachings I had been giving her. My first reaction was anger, then embarrassment, then guilt. I immediately began to blame myself, saying things like, It's my fault. I began to question myself. Where did I go wrong? I starting saying things like, I should have been a better parent, I should have done it differently.

Most parents act the same way. They blame themselves for their children's misbehavior. They go on what we call guilt trips, which prevents them from seeing the unseen influence that is actually behind the attitude and actions of their children. This influence is none other than Satan, the ruler of all evil and wicked spirits. The parents fail to realize that their children could be operating under the spirits of rebellion and disobedience and that they need to take authority over those spirits and bind up those spirits.

I was guilty; I was ignorant of the devil's devices. I was ignorant of the fact that while I was spending time worrying, and grieving over things I could see with my natural eyes, Satan and his controlling forces were free to carry out their operations in the life of my child. What I should have done instead of worrying and blaming myself was to pray! I found out that prayer is a hindrance to Satan's work. I should have been interceding on her behalf. I should have been praying against the forces of darkness that were in operation in my child's life like never before.

This was a very critical time for her. She had opened the door to Satan, and he was determined to destroy her. She needed my prayers.

I became so self-centered and so overwhelmed with how people would look at me, because of the way my child was behaving that I failed to recognize the controlling forces in her life and that she needed help.

Not long ago my daughter told me something that really started me thinking. She said, "Mamie, if parents could remember how they were when they were growing up (their mind set at the time) they would be better able to understand their children and it would be much easier for them to relate to the things their children are going through." I admit sometimes I do forget.

Children today are undergoing a tremendous amount of pressure from all forces of life, that some of us did not have to deal with when we were growing up. I believe one of the greatest tools Satan uses to influence our children today is the media. It is one of his greatest tools of this century. Most family coverage by the media diminishes family values and teaches children disrespect for parents and adults. They paint a false picture of how a family is truly supposed to be. Most of the coverage is against religious family teachings, like obedience, respect for others and the elderly, and honor to parents. Such coverage has a very negative influence on your child. This is why it is a must that parents monitor what their children watch on TV, take time to view programs with their children and discuss those programs from a godly standpoint.

Another tool Satan uses against your child is peer pressure. I believe the main reason teens become involved in improper sexual activities, drugs, alcohol, gangs and other inappropriate behavior is because of peer pressure.

It is important that parents spend quality time with their children, teaching and helping them understand what true friendship is all about. A child has to understand that a true friend does not cause either harm or hurt to come to his friend. A true friend cares about the well-being of his friend. He does not give his friend wrong advice. Don't be afraid to observe your child's friends closely. Get to know the children your child is associating with.

You ask, "How do I get to know them?" Do something special for your child and ask him to invite his friends over. When his friends are around, periodically talk with them and get a sense of where they are, get to know them. Do not be naive.

Children today are not like they were when we were growing up. Kids today are into a lot more than we ever dreamed of when we were kids. Things we were afraid to do, kids today do without thinking twice about it. This is why it is vital that you clearly discuss what is acceptable and right behaviors based on your morals, values and beliefs. Parents have to encourage their children to carefully choose their friends. Children should be encouraged to choose friends based on their values, their religious beliefs and their outlook of life. A parent needs the wisdom of God in helping their children deal with the attacks Satan brings against them through surrounding influences. How does a parent gain this wisdom? By asking God for it.

> *"If any of you lack wisdom, let him ask of God, that giveth to all men liberally, and upbraideth not; and it shall be given him."*
>
> (James 1:5)

If you are feeling sorry for yourself, as I was, because of your child's wrong behavior, God does not want you doing that. He does not want you going on guilt trips and placing the blame on yourself. He does not want you feeling embarrassed or ashamed, instead, He wants you to seek His wisdom and guidance through prayer. He also wants you to muster every ounce of energy you have to pray against Satan and his host of controlling forces.

If you find yourself getting tired and weak, call on other believers who can help you pray for your child. Do as Moses did. He used the same tactics against the Amalekites, and it worked. Chapter 17 of Exodus gives an account of the children of Israel in battle against the Amalekites, in order for the children of Israel to win the battle, Moses had to stand up on the top of a hill with the staff of God in his hands and his hands stretched out toward heaven. The Bible says as long as Moses kept his hands up, the Israelites were winning. When Moses's hands got tired and he lowered his hands the enemy began to win. Therefore, Aaron and Hur got a stone for Moses to sit on, and they held his hands up to prevent the Amalekites from winning the battle.

There are times when the burden may become so overwhelming for you that you feel like you want to give up. Parents, please don't give up and lose the battle. Do as Moses did, call on a Hur and an Aaron, let them hold up your arms in prayer. Call on some trustworthy believers, let them intercede in prayer for that son or that daughter, and rest assured that you will win the battle. There is power in prayer.

I remember another occasion when I felt very discouraged about my daughter's actions. I began to really cry out to God for His intervention in her life. I had people everywhere interceding for her.

One night at about 1:00 a.m., I received a phone call from a friend. She sounded very excited. She had some good news to share with me, and she couldn't wait to tell me. She began by saying, "Elizabeth, as I was praying for your daughter, the Lord gave me words regarding your child. The Lord wants you to know that He has already mapped out your daughter's life. He wants you to know He has selected her as one of His fruitful servants, she shall bring forth many fruits, good fruits and men shall eat of her fruits."

Be encouraged! God is in control of the situation. Your child will come to know the Lord. She will serve Him. He has heard your prayers, He has heard your secret cries, He has seen your tears. He has never left you neither has He forsaken you. He has already solved the problem. In other words, before you even thought of praying, before your daughter was ever thought of, before she was even conceived, God already knew her, sanctified her and had good plans for her life.

Those were encouraging words to me. I believe the Lord gave her those words to remind me and to assure me once again of His promises to me concerning my child. Everything the Lord had said to me regarding my daughter's future, confirmed the revelation my friend received that night about my daughter.

You see, I had allowed myself to become so overwhelmed and engrossed in her wrong doings that I closed my eyes and my mind to all of the promises of God concerning my child. Instead of spending time in prayer professing God's promises for my child and taking authority over the controlling forces in her life, I allowed myself to focus on her actions. But because of God's love and mercy, He still reminded me of His promises for her even in the midst of my self-pity and encouraged me not to give up.

I am constantly learning to go through the Word of God to find His promises and pray them for my daughter. I am confident that God's Word never fails. He assured me that His Word will never return unto Him void, but it will accomplish what He pleases.

> *"So shall my Word be that goeth forth out of my mouth; it shall not return unto me void, but it shall accomplish that which I please, and it shall prosper in the thing whereto I sent it."* (Isaiah 55:11)

Your child may not be heading in the direction of the Lord at this time, but remember God's Word and hold on to His promises for you. In God's own appointed time, believe that your child will come to know the Lord.

I have heard some Christian parents of little children criticize other Christian parents with troubled children, saying unkind things such as: "If that parent had reared that child up right, if that parent had prayed like he should have, if that parent had done what he should have done, that child would have not gone astray. He calls himself a man of God, she calls herself a woman of God, but why are their children behaving like that?"

To those critics, just in case you have not had the experience or you really do not understand some of the avenues Satan uses to bring embarrassment to God's people. I want you to know that Satan will use whoever allows himself to be used to bring shame to the name of Jesus. He will use the children of ministers, church leaders, evangelist, Sunday School teachers, other mighty men and women of God, if those children avail themselves to Satan to be used by him.

This does not necessarily mean those parents did not do their job in rearing their children. It could very well be that those children opened the door to Satan to use them as his tools in bringing shame to the ministry and people of God. As I said, Satan will use whoever allows him. To those critics I also say, hold your comments until your own children are grown up. If you have no problems with any of them, then give God the glory. For it is by His grace and sovereignty you have been spared the burden of dealing with an estranged child. Don't criticize, pray for those who are struggling with troubled children. They need your prayers.

Just because a parent has an estranged child does not necessarily mean he did not do a good job rearing his child. On the other hand, just because you never had to deal with a troubled child does not necessarily means you are a better parent than a parent who had a troubled child. I have heard of godly parents, praying parents, parents who love the

Lord with all their hearts tell stories of the many struggles they experienced with some of their children.

These struggles did not come because the parents were weak or not good, or not firm parents, or because the parents didn't love the Lord. Some of these parents probably did their best at the time to rear godly children. They probably did their best to teach their children in the way of the Lord, but the children decided to obey another voice. You have to realize that as long as Satan is in this world, there will be struggles, there will be attacks, there will be tribulations, there will be afflictions, but praise be to God, through His Son Jesus Christ, you have victory over every situation that comes your way.

I have also heard some of those same parents who have struggled many years with their troubled children give testimonies, relating how God miraculously transformed those troubled children into men and women of God. These parents have testified that those same children are beautifully serving God today. Some of them are, pastors, teachers, youth leaders, evangelists, and missionaries; now in the ministry, working for the Lord. In all things God is working to bring glory to His name!

You may not understand why God allowed certain things to occur in your life, but God is God. He knows all things, His ways are beyond finding out.

> *"O the depth of the riches both of the wisdom and knowledge of God! How unsearchable are His judgements, and His ways past finding out."* (Romans 11:38)

The wisdom and knowledge of God are much greater than that of humanity. The depths of God's wisdom are far beyond man's ability to comprehend them. Just know without a doubt that whatever God allows in your life will lead to good results.

Parents, do not get me wrong, I am not saying that all Christian parents do a good job in rearing their children. A lot of parents have blown it. A lot of parents have made many mistakes in child rearing. A lot of parents somewhere along the way lost track of their God-given parenting responsibility. There are parents who have not been godly examples to their children. They have not followed God's child-rearing manuscript, the Bible, in rearing their children. They have not followed Scriptures like:

> *"Train up a child in a way he should go: when he is old, he will not depart from it."*
> (Proverbs 22:6)

> *"Foolishness is bound in the heart of a child: but the rod of correction will drive it far from him."* (Proverb 13:24)

> *"He that spareth his rod hateth his son: but he that loveth him chasteneth him betimes."*
> (Proverbs 13:24)
> *"Withhold not correction from the child: if thou beatest him with the rod, He shall not die. Thou shalt beat him with the rod, and shalt deliver his soul from hell."*
> (Proverbs 23:13-14)

*"And, ye fathers, provoke not your children
to wrath: but bring them up in the nurture
and admonition of the Lord."*

(Ephesians 6:4)

These and many other Scriptures parents may have been guilty of not following when it comes to child rearing. Some parents are guilty of not disciplining their children in Love, instead, they have used the rod in anger and harshness, which have left some children emotional scared. Some may have not been the loving parents God has called them to be. Some have not been around when their children needed them. Some have been abusive parents. Some were too busy moving up the corporate ladder and lost sight of their children's needs.

I also believe that for those parents who have blown it, and which they could do it all over again, and have asked God forgiveness and are working on being better parents, God is sovereign, and merciful and can turn those situations around to bring glory to Him. As you continue to labor in prayer for your lost children, God will hear your prayers and draw those children unto Him.

I believe the words I received that night from my dear friend who was interceding on behalf of my daughter, were not just for me, I believe those words were for every parent who has concerns about his child's spiritual growth.

As you read this book, God is assuring you once again that He has plans for your child.

Chapter 5

CARRYING UNNECESSARY BURDENS

Sometimes people allow themselves to become so burdened with life's trials that they forget to look to God, who is the fixer of every situation that appears hopeless. They allow themselves to endure unnecessary burdens only because they fail to exercise the Word of God in their daily walk.

God says in Psalm 55:22, *"Cast your burden upon the Lord, and He shall sustain thee: He shall never suffer the righteous to be moved."*

Whatever hardship God allows His people to experience, He sustains them through it. Like the rooted tree that is swayed back and forth in the storm and still stands, so shall God sustain the righteous. They may be disturbed, sometimes distressed, but they shall never be uprooted.

God did not design your body to carry burdens. The weight of a burden is too great for you to bear. You are not skilled to deal with all of life's problems. This is why God told you to turn them over to Him. The Hebrew word for cast is "*Shalak*," which means to throw out or throw away. When you throw something away, you are indicating that you are through with it. You do not usually go back and get it. God wants you to do the same with your cares: throw them on Him, never to retrieve them. He is much better equipped to handle them than you are.

I Peter 5:7 tells you to cast all your cares upon the Lord, for He cares for you. That verse did not say cast all except those that have to do with your child. It said "ALL"; all your cares, all your anxieties, all your burdens, all your worries. God has a personal concern for you. He desires that you be free of all anxieties and have peace of mind. When you hold on to your burdens, God cannot do anything about them. He cannot help you with them, because He does not have them. You have them. They are still in your possession. God will never force you to turn your burdens over to Him. He will allow you to carry them until you learn to turn them over to Him.

Whenever you allow yourself to become worried or burdened over the way you see your child acting, instead of doing something about it and turning the rest over to the Lord for His intervention, what you are in essence telling the Lord is, "I can handle this situation by myself. I don't need your help." In so doing, you completely shut God out from intervening on your behalf. You prevent Him from helping you with the situation.

In order for God to come in, and give you peace and guidance in what you are going through, you must give the entire situation to Him. He will give you directions, if you do allow Him. He is by your side, ready to help.

One of the things I have learned over the years is, whenever I try to take matters in my own hands, instead of turning them over to God, they end up in disaster.

Learn to lean on God for His guidance in dealing with your children's rebellious behaviors, and do not carry needless burdens. Unnecessary worries and burdens are products of human untrusting nature and they can lead to self-destruction. Please do not get me wrong, I am not saying that God will take all of the problems out of your life, because I do understand that much of what happens in your life is God ordained for your spiritual growth, remember that God is there to help you with your "hardheaded" children.

God said in Psalm 46:10a, *"Be still, and know that I am God."* He desires that you know Him even as you know your name. You may say, "How do I get to know God in such a fashion?"

Well, you get to know God through studying His Word. When you know God, it becomes easy to trust Him. He desires that you know that He is at work in every aspect of your life. He is perfecting all the things that concern you.

> *"The Lord will perfect that which concerneth me: Thy mercy O Lord, endureth forever: forsake not the works of thine hands."* (Psalm 138:8)

Believe God's Word and know that His ability exceeds your imagination. As you learn of the Lord, you will begin to experience the joy of the Lord, and you will find the strength you need to wait on Him. He will encourage you and you will find hope in Him. He knows your strengths and your weaknesses. He is very much aware of how much you are able to bear.

When you reach the point where you can't take any more and want to give up, by His divine guidance, He will speak to your heart to strengthen you as you wait. He may speak to you through His Word, a friend, by way of radio, television or through some sort of written material. Regardless of what means He chooses, He will give you just the right words you need to regain courage to continue. God's timing is perfect. He never fails to amaze me of His timeliness.

It happens to me all the time. Just when I feel like all hope is gone and I am on the verge of giving up, out of nowhere, He sends someone by with just the right words to encourage me and lift up my spirit. I am amazed by some of the means the Lord uses to speak to my heart. He uses words on stickers on the back of someone's car. He uses words on posters, on flyers, and many other means. Let me tell you about two incidents that come quickly to mind in which God spoke so clearly to me.

Not too long ago, someone made me so angry, I felt like I could explode. I was driving down the street, mad as I could be. All of a sudden, I found myself behind a car that had a large sticker displayed on its bumper. It read, "RELAX, GOD IS IN CONTROL." I couldn't help but laugh. And the peace of God just overwhelmed my heart.

On another occasion, a person I thought I knew, did some hurtful things to me, I was really upset over the situation. I decided to get even with that person for what he did to me. I had given up hope that God would intervene for me, and I thought, if He was going to, He was taking too long. I had my plans all worked out of how I was going to get even with this person. I allowed myself to get so angry that the thought of forgiving this person never crossed my mind.

A friend pulled up alongside me at a gas station. I went over to her car to speak to her. She seemed excited and said, "Let me show you what I have been doing in my spare time." She pulled out a video and showed it to me, and said, "Look what I've been watching." The title of the video was, "FORGIVE."

When I got back to my car, the Lord began to minister to my heart. He said, "That is what I want you to do for that person who hurt you, "Forgive that person." I asked God to give me the strength to do that. I felt in my strength it was impossible for me to do. With God's help, I was able to forgive that person. I felt much better.

God is sovereign. He speaks to His children all the time, even in the midst of their many trying circumstances. If you will only stop for a moment and listen, you will hear God's encouraging and uplifting words to you. If you have not been able to hear the voice of the Lord, you probably have allowed yourself to become so overwhelmed with the situation, that you miss your opportunity to hear the Lord speaking to you.

Parents after you have done all you can with your child and nothing seems to work, turn him over to God and trust that He is in control of his life. He will work out the situation. Nothing is impossible with God.

Chapter 6

BELIEVING EVEN
WHEN IT SEEMS IMPOSSIBLE

Sometimes you have to see God's Word in action before you can believe it. God requires that His people believe His Word even if the situation appears impossible. When you believe that God can move in an impossible situation, you are excising faith in God. This frees God to work that situation out for you and causes Him to put things in order for the resolution of the impossible situation.

The Bible says, *"But without faith it is impossible to please Him: for he that cometh to God must believe that He is, and that He is a rewarder to them that diligently seek Him."* (Hebrews 11:6)

Thomas, one of the twelve disciples of Jesus, did not believe the report of the other disciples when they told him that they had seen the Lord after He was crucified. His response to them was, *"except I shall see in His hands the print of the nails, and put my finger into the print of the nail, and thrust my hand into His side, I will not believe."*

(John 20:25-29)

Our Lord Jesus Christ is pleased with us when we demonstrate faith in His Word by believing although we have not yet seen change in the situation. When you began to walk by faith and not by sight, when you say in your heart, "Lord, this situation seems impossible, I just don't know what to do and cannot see how this can be turned around, but Lord, I know You are able to do all things because you are Omnipotent, All Powerful God, nothing is impossible for you to do, I know you can turn my child around," I really believe the Lord will prove Himself faithful to you.

I encourage you to search God's Word and find out what God is saying concerning you and your child. Find out what promises He made to your child, write those promises down, and when you pray, remind God of His promises. It's okay to remind God; He told us to do so.

> *"Put me in remembrance: let us plead together: declare thou, that thou mayest be justified."* (Isaiah 43:26)

It is God's desire to bring His Word to pass.

> *"So shall My Word be that goeth forth out of my mouth: it shall not return unto me void, but it shall accomplish that which I please, and it shall prosper in the things whereto I sent it."* (Isaiah 55:11)

Not only does God send His Word forth, but He

watches over it to perform it. If God made a promise to you, believe Him. He will surely bring it to pass. As you read the Word of God, and embrace it, and personalize it, God will reveal Himself to you in an awesome way. If you will dare to believe God's Word, it will work on your behalf.

Chapter 7

COMBATING THE FORCES
OF DARKNESS

"For the weapons of our warfare are not carnal, but mighty through God to the pulling down of strong holds."
(II Corinthians 10:4)

Satan has already been defeated. His work has already been destroyed.

"For this purpose the Son of God was manifested, that He might destroy the works of the devil."
(I John 3:8)

Because of what Christ has already done for you, you have nothing to fear. Through Christ's death on the cross, you gain victory over all the works of Satan. Christ has already destroyed Satan's work.

Romans 8:37 tells us that we are more than conquerors, meaning Christ has done the work for us. He has given us the benefits to enjoy. When you begin to truly believe this, you will have more peace and you will be relieved from needless worrying about Satan winning the battle.

You see, Christ has already won the battle for you. There is no need for you to panic when you are confronted with attacks from Satan and his forces. The problem is that whenever you are experiencing problems with your child and you feel that you are losing the battle, you are focusing on the problem, which prohibits you from seeing spiritually the controlling forces that are behind your child's actions. In the process, you lose sight of God's power, and fail to see His intervention in the whole matter. This can cause you to become spiritually blind and prevent you from seeing the outstretched arm of God covering your child from Satan's destructive forces.

Recognize God in every situation and learn to praise Him by faith for what He is doing in the spiritual realm on your behalf that you cannot see with your natural eyes. When a situation gets out of control for you, remember, it is not out of control for God. What you consider to be a hopeless case is just the ideal case God wants to use to bring glory to Him.

I am reminded of Daniel in the Old Testament who prayed, mourned and fasted for His people. I believe he sensed in his heart that God did not hear his prayers the first time he prayed. He continued praying and fasting for twenty-one days. What Daniel didn't know was that the first day he prayed, God heard him and sent a messenger down to him with his answer. The prince of Persia, (one of Satan's agents) detained the messenger for three weeks to prevent him from relaying God's message to Daniel. There is spiritual warfare going on in the heavenlies of which very little is known on the earth. God, in His sovereignty, afforded a little glimpse of it in Daniel Chapter 10.

If it was not for the mercy of God and His shield of protection over your child, Satan would have long since destroyed him. John 10:10 says, *"The thief cometh not, but to steal, and to kill, and to destroy: I am come that they might have life, and that they might have it more abundantly."*

Satan is a thief, He wants to steal your child from God, kill him in hope to destroy all of God's plans for his life. Satan does not want your child serving God. As you fervently pray for your child, God will not allow Satan's desires to come upon him, although God may allow situations in your child's life, to awaken him and cause him to come to his senses to get on the right track with Him.

Keep in mind also that Satan sometimes attacks your loved ones to get to you. He despises the fact that you have chosen to live a godly lifestyle. He does everything he can to prevent that from happening. He attacks through any means available to him.

He usually comes through the closest people to you, who sometimes happen to be your children. He works through them, he manipulates them and causes them to do things contrary to the way of God with the intent of bringing discouragement to you, so that you can give up and turn your back on God. In this way, he will be free to destroy your children.

Over the years, I have learned to run to God during times when I am experiencing my strongest attacks, and God has never failed me yet. He has always seen me through and delivered me out of my trouble. Please do not get discouraged, do not get weary, instead run to the Lord. He will be your helper, He will deliver you and your loved ones as you persevere in prayer.

It is imperative that you study God's word, and know it. If you have a problem understanding the Word of God, pray and ask Him to give you understanding and revelation of His Word. It is important that you know who you are in the Lord.

> *"This book of the law shall not depart from thy mouth; but thou shall meditate in it day and night, that thou mayest observe to do according to all that is written therein; For by them thou shall make thy way prosperous, and by them thou shall have good success."* (Joshua 1:8)

Also ask the Lord to give you the strength you need to stand against Satan's attacks. There is power in prayer. Tremendous amounts of damage can be done to Satan kingdom through your prayer. God has already given you the weapon you need to use against Satan and his forces.

No believer should allow the devil the privilege of gaining an upper hand over him. Instead, he should use his God-given authority to overcome Satan.

There is no reason why children of God should be

manipulated or intimidated by Satan, especially when they know the Word of God. A child of God has no business allowing Satan to overcome him. Do not put yourself in a sad, and depressed frame of mind because of what you see with the natural eye. Christ has destroyed all of Satan's work on Calvary, plus He has given you power over him.

In Luke 10:19, Christ says, *"Behold, I give unto you power to tread on serpents and scorpions, and over all the power of the enemy, and nothing shall by any means hurt you."*

You cannot allow the enemy to use your mind as his brewing field for promoting negativism about you or your child. Do not entertain his lies. Start speaking what God says into the life of your child. Exercise the power and authority God has given you by praying against the work of Satan.

Jesus took no foolishness from the devil. He knew that Satan was a no good, defeated foe. Jesus knew Satan's end. When Satan tried to control Jesus through manipulation, Jesus used the Word to put him in his place. Luke 4:1-13, *"...IT IS WRITTEN... GET THEE BEHIND ME Satan."*

Be imitators of Jesus. He never entertained Satan's foolishness. He always used the Word to put Satan in his place, "behind Him." Learn to use the Word of God against the enemy. Speak the Word. When the enemy tells you that your child won't amount to anything, you look him right in the eye and tell him. "It is written me and my house shall be saved; my child will be saved. It is written! Devil, my child shall be taught of the Lord, and great shall be his peace. The Word also says, the fruit of my womb is His reward. My child is God's reward."

Use the Word. The Word is your weapon against the enemy. You will overcome Satan by the Word. The Word will set you free. Don't be afraid to use it. God's Word must accomplish its purpose.

> *"For though we walk in the flesh, we do not war after the flesh."*
>
> (II Corinthians 10:3)

> *"For we wrestle not against flesh and blood. But against principalities, and against powers, against rulers of darkness of this world, against spiritual wickedness in high places."* (Ephesians 6:12)

Although you are in a battle with unseen forces, God had instructed you on how to be strong and stand against the wiles of the devil in order to win the battle. He said in Ephesians Chapter 6 to put on the whole armor of God. The armor of God is your protection against the forces that seek to destroy you.

> *"Wherefore take unto you the whole armor of God, that ye may be able to withstand in the evil day, and having done all, to stand. Stand therefore, having your loins girt about with truth, and having on the breast plate of righteousness;*
> *And your feet shod with the preparation of the gospel of peace;*

Above all taking the shield of faith,
wherewith ye shall be able to quench all
the fiery darts of the wicked.
And take the helmet of salvation, and the
sword of the Spirit, which is the Word of
God:"   (Ephesians 6:13-17)

"For the weapons of our warfare are not
carnal but mighty through God for the
pulling down of strongholds."
                            (II Corinthians 10:4)

God has given you mighty weapons by which to defeat the enemy, I believe He wants you to use them. Instead of pleading, fussing, arguing, and fighting with your child start using your authority against the controlling forces behind your child's actions.

Children are driven by spirits of lying, spirits of disobedience, rebellious, running away spirits, etc. These are all demonic. God has given you the authority to bind and cast out those forces.

"Verily I say unto you, whatsoever ye shall
bind on earth shall be bound in Heaven:
and whatsoever ye shall loose on earth,
shall be loosed in heaven."   (Matt. 18:18)

"And these signs shall follow them that
believe; In my name shall they cast out
devils...."   (Mark 16:17a)

God has given you the weapons you need. It's time to stop looking at the problems and start doing something about them.

No matter how hopeless you may think the situation is, never, never give up hope in your child. Satan desires that you give up, he desires that you stop praying. He would like to see you stop warring against his forces of darkness. You see, without your prayers, Satan is free to succeed in his plans for destroying you and your child. Please do not give him that privilege. Stay before God, pray, and come against Satan's forces.

Be mindful of the types of words you use on your child. Words are powerful, they can have lasting effects. Your words can have either a negative effect or a positive effect. They can be uplifting or detrimental.

The Bible says, *"Death and life are in the power of the tongue..."* (Proverbs 18:21a)

You can speak life to your child by the words you use or you can speak death to him.

Many children are scarred today because of negative words with which they have been bombarded by their parents and others. Some parents call their children names like "stupid" and "dumb" all the time and as a result, these children grow up stereotyped, thinking that they are stupid and/or dumb and they act accordingly. Some parents get angry or frustrated with their children and say words like "You will not amount to anything." After hearing this for so long, the children begin to believe that what their parents said about them is true. Therefore, they begin losing all interest and desire to achieve. You see, negative words have a psychological effect on the mind. Be very careful with the choice of words you use on your child. You are the parent, your child trusts and believes what you say.

Be the encouraging force in your child's life. It is important that you speak positively to your child. All day long, your child is confronted with various kinds of negative, discouraging, and diminishing words, when he comes home, he needs your support. When people call him "dumb" and tell him, he won't make it, he needs to hear you counteract those negative statements with positive, encouraging and uplifting ones, "Honey you can make it, I believe in you, I have confidence in your ability to succeed."

I can recall many occasions when my daughter would come to me and say, "Mamie, no matter how hard I try, it seems like I can't do anything right, I tried, but I just can't do it." She would be ready to give up. What she was in essence communicating to me was, "Mamie, I need your help, I need your support." She needed to hear me say, "Honey, you can do it, I know you can." She needed some encouraging words that would help make her feel better about what she was trying to do. I felt that it was important that I give her the right support that she needed.

From prior experiences which included mistakes, I knew my response could cause her to press harder or cause her to give up. I definitely did not want her giving up. I did my best to encourage her to believe that she has the capability to succeed in anything she puts her mind to do.

I knew that God had already given that to her, and she had to know it too. I didn't just stop at giving her words of encouragement, I also helped to make what she was doing less complicated. I worked with her in the areas she had difficulties, and if I had no knowledge in that area, I sought help either from friends, books at home, or from the library. Don't get me wrong, I am not saying take over your child's responsibilities, all I am saying is if you see that your child is trying and giving the situation his best effort, but just can't seem to get it right, do your best to help him.

If you have been a parent who is constantly speaking negative words to your child, causing him to feel down, low and hurt, stop as of this day and ask God to forgive you. Then ask God to help you change your thinking so you can use the ability He has given you to speak words of life to your child instead of words of death.

Chapter 8

BEING KNOWLEDGABLE
OF GOD'S PROMISES

God provided various verses in His Word to assure you that your child can succeed, he can make it, and it is God's will that your child be saved. I have discussed some of those verses and I will be exploring more of God's promises for your child. God desires that you know without any doubt that He wants to see your child prosper in all things. In order for you to believe God's promises, in order for you to be able to exercise faith that those promises will come to pass, you must know them. If you don't know them, you really have nothing to hold on to. This causes you to struggle with situations that God has already promised to make you victorious in. Take time and search the Scriptures to find more of God's promises.

As a believer, the promises God made to Abraham concerning him and his seed belong to you also. You came under the covenant God made to Abraham and became entitled to the blessings with which God blessed Abraham when you accepted Jesus Christ as your Lord and Savior.

> *"Christ has redeemed us from the curse of the Law, being made a curse for us: it is written, cursed is everyone that hangeth on the tree:*
>
> *That the BLESSING of Abraham might come on the gentiles (us) THROUGH JESUS CHRIST; that we might receive the promise of the Spirit through faith."*
>
> (Galatians 3:13-14)

Through Jesus Christ, you are the offspring of Abraham. Therefore, you being of the seed of Abraham, God sees you as a blessed person. God intends that your child be a blessed child also. He views your child in an awesome way. He sees your child as His heritage and His reward.

> *"Lo, children are an heritage of the Lord: and the fruit of the womb are His reward."*
>
> (Psalm 127:3)

You have to begin to see your child as Jesus sees him. He sees your child as His little one whom He desires to come to Him.

> *"Jesus said, suffer the little children, and forbid them not to come unto me: for of such is the kingdom of Heaven."*
>
> (Matt. 19:4)

When you begin to look at your child the way Jesus sees him, you will see him differently. Don't spend time looking at the things your child does in the natural and not enough time praying and believing that God will hear your prayers and touch your child's heart to turn to Him. And that those wrong behaviors will be used as testimonies that will bring glory to God.

Start believing God's promises by faith and know that your child will come to know God and walk in the way God would have him.

> *"Now faith is the substance of things hoped*
> *for the evidence of things not seen."*
> (Hebrews 11:1)

Start hoping that your child will come to know the Lord, even when there is no sign of evidence that he would. When you believe anything other than what God says in His Word, you are showing lack of faith and trust in Him. Abraham was greatly blessed by God, because He believed God's Word. Although he did not see everything that God promised, by faith, He believed God, and patiently waited to see the promise come to pass. (Hebrew 6:13-15)

As you exercise that same kind of faith Abraham demonstrated in God, and wait patiently on God to complete His work in your child's life, you will obtain the fullness of His blessings and you will see the manifestation of His promises in the life of your child.

Promises God made millions of years ago are for today. His Word never changes. His Word has been proven over the years by millions of believers to be true. His Word will work in your life today if you can believe by faith. As you continue in the way of God, you will experience God's hand in that situation and you will see a turn around for the best. His Word is for today and it is for your child also. Jesus assures us in Matthew 24:35,

> *"Heaven and earth may pass away,*
> *but my Word will not pass away."*

What He says, stands! God is not fickle, He does not play games, He is genuine in all His ways. People change, circumstances change, environments change, friends change, but God's Word never changes. His Word is established forever. He will perform what He says all the time. God is searching for people who will dare to believe, so He can manifest His strength and power through their lives. Can you be that people today?

No matter what you are going through with your son or daughter, don't give up, trust God. He is faithful. Your suffering is not in vain. God will work that situation out for you. Know without a doubt that God loves you and He will perfect those things that concern you. The same covenant God established with Abraham, He also established with you.

> *"And I will establish my covenant between*
> *me and thee and thou seed after thee in*
> *their generations for an everlasting*
> *covenant, to be a God unto thee and to thy*
> *seed after thee."* (Genesis 17:7)

> *"For all of the land which thou seest, to*
> *thee will I give it, and to thy seed forever.*
> *And I will make thou seed as the dust of the*

earth; so that if a man can number the dust of the earth, then shall thy seed be numbered." (Genesis 13:15,16)

According to the above passage, God will be a God to you *and to your seed*. All of the blessings God has for you, He also desires to give them to your child.

"And I will give unto thee, and to thy seed after thee the land wherein thou art stranger, all the land of Canaan, for an everlasting possession; and I will be their God." (Genesis 17:8)

"And thy seed shalt be as the dust of the earth, and thou shalt spread abroad to the west, and the east, and to the north, and to the south: and in thy seed shall all the families of the earth be blessed." (Genesis 28:14)

"That in blessing I will bless thee, and in multiplying I will multiply thy seed as the stars of the heaven and as the sand which is upon the sea shore; and thy seed shall possess the gate of his enemy.

And in thy seed shall all the nations of the earth be blessed; because thou hast obeyed my voice."

When you obey God, there is nothing He will not do for you. Out of obedience comes the blessings of God. This blessing is not only for you but God extends it to your child.

> *"And the land which I gave Abraham and Isaac, to thee will I give it, and to thy seed after thee will I give the land."*
>
> (Genesis 35:12)

> *"But with thee will I establish my covenant; and thou shalt come in the ark, and thy sons, and thy wife, and thy sons' wives with thee."* (Genesis 6:18)

God promised that you will come into the ark; God's ark of safety from the storms of life, from the rain, from the heat of the sun, from the forces of darkness, from the attacks of the enemy, from the struggles and burdens of life. God promised to hide you and your child in His ark a place of protection!

> *"And yet for all that, when they be in the land of their enemies, I will not cast them away, neither will I abhor them, to destroy them utterly, and to break my covenant with them: for I am the Lord their God.*
>
> *But I will for their sakes remember the covenant of their ancestors, whom I brought from forth out of the land of Egypt in the sight of the heathen, that I might be their God: I am the Lord."*
>
> (Leviticus 26:44,45)

"And because He loved thy fathers, therefore he chose their seed after them, and brought thee out in his sight with his mighty power out of Egypt."

(Deuteronomy 4:15)

"Only the Lord had a delight in thy fathers to love them, and He chose their seed after them, even you above all people, as it is this day." (Deuteronomy 10:15)

"Observe and hear all there words which I commend thee, that it may go well with thee, and with thy children after thee forever, when thou doest that which is good and right in the sight of the Lord thy God."

(Deuteronomy 12:28)

"I have been young, not I am old; yet have I not seen the righteous forsaken, his seed begging bread.
He is ever merciful, and lendeth; and his seed is blessed." (Psalm 37:25,26)

Parents, these are powerful verses to hold on to. These promises are for you.

"The children of thy servants shall continue. And their seed shall be established before thee." (Psalm 102:28)

"But the mercy of the Lord is from everlasting to everlasting on them that fear Him and His righteousness unto children's children." (Psalm 103:17)

"Praise the Lord, blessed is the man that feareth the Lord, that delighteth greatly in His commandment.

His seed shall be mighty upon the earth: the generation of the upright shall be blessed.

Wealth and riches shall be in his house: and his righteousness endureth for ever."
(Psalm 112:1-3)

According to the Word of God, if you will reverence God, if you will fear and honor Him, if you will delight greatly in his commandment, He will see to it that your child becomes mighty on the earth. This is His Word, if He says it, He will do it, so expect it.

"Thou join hand in hand, the wicked shall not be unpunished: but the seed of the righteous shall be delivered."
(Proverbs 11:21)

Though the wicked come together against you, against your child, they will not get away with it. They will be punished and God will deliver your child.

"The just man walketh in His integrity: His children are blessed after him."
(Proverbs 20:7)

"Children's children are the crown of old man; and the glory of children are their fathers." (Psalm 17:6)

"As arrow are in the hand of a mighty man; so are children of the youth.
Happy is the man who hath his quiver full of them, they shall not be ashamed, but they shall speak with the enemies in the gate."
(Psalm 127:4-5)

"Thy children are like olive plants round about thy table." (Psalm 128:3b)

"For I will pour water upon him that is thirsty, and floods upon the dry ground: I will pour my Spirit upon thy seed, and my blessing upon thy offspring;
And thou shall spring up as among the grass, as willows by the water courses."
(Isaiah 44:3,4)

"For thou shall break forth on the right and on the left; and thy seed shall inherit the Gentiles, and make the desolate cities to be inhabited.
And all thy children shall be taught of the

Lord; and great shall be the peace of thy
children." (Isaiah 44:3,4)

Believe these promises for your child. When you go to
God in prayer on behalf of your child, pray the Word of
God, His Word works. God always performs His Word.

"They shall not labor in vain, not bring
forth for trouble: for they are the seed of the
blessed of the Lord, and their offspring with
them." (Isaiah 65:23)

Pray like this: "Father, you said, that I shall not labor
in vain, You said, that I shall not bring forth for trouble.
This is your Word Lord, so I thank you that my labor is not
in vain and my child was not brought forth for trouble. I
thank you that my child is of the seed of the blessed of the
Lord."

"Before I formed thee in the belly I knew
thee; and before thou comest forth out of
the womb I sanctified thee...."
(Jeremiah 1:5a,b)

"Then Peter said unto them, repent and be
baptized every one of you in the name of
Jesus Christ for the remission of sins, and
ye shall receive the gift of the Holy Ghost.
For the promise is unto you and your
children, and to all that are afar off, even as
many as the Lord our God shall call."
(Acts 2:38,39)

God has also promised your child the gift of the Holy Spirit through Jesus Christ. If you want your child to do what is right, and walk in the right path, then pray that you child give his life to Christ and receive the gift of the Holy Spirit which God so freely offers. You see, when the Holy Spirit comes in, he teaches, directs, guides and instills all truth. Your child will know the truth. He will be lead in the right way as he follows the leading of the Holy Spirit. The Holy Spirit also brings with him His fruits which are: love, joy, peace, longsuffering, gentleness, goodness, faithfulness, meekness and temperance.

The Holy Spirit will teach your child how to love others, how to experience joy on the inside, even when things on the outside don't look so joyous. He will help your child to experience peace, even when things around him looks chaotic. The Holy Spirit will teach Him how to be gentle, meek or teachable, how to wait on the Lord and how to walk in temperance.

Continue in prayer, There is nothing prayer cannot do. Do what God told the children of Israel to do in Isaiah 62:7:

"I have set watchmen on your walls, O Jerusalem; They shall never hold their peace day or night. You who make mention of the Lord, do not keep silent, and give Him no rest till He establishes and till He makes Jerusalem a praise in the earth."

Persevere for your child. You are that "watchman" God has set over your children, give God no rest until you see your child saved, walking in holiness and in the fear of

God; until you see your child a praise in the earth. God is faithful!

So far, I have listed just few of the promises God has made to you and your child. As you continue to search the Scriptures, you will find more. Believe God for those promises and claim them for your child. Your child is blessed of God. You may be facing difficult times with your child now, please don't look at things in the natural, look at them in the spirit. As you do your part in obeying God and leading your child in the way of the Lord, expect God to do the impossible. God has decreed and has established His Word. He said your child is His heritage and the fruit of your womb is His reward. God has a purpose for all children including yours, that will bring glory to Him.

> *"And they said, believe on the Lord Jesus Christ and thou shalt be saved, and thou household."* (Acts 16:31)

There are those who will read this verse and say, "my child no longer lives with me, therefore he is not a part of my household." The location of your child does not make a difference. Your child moving out of your house does not destroy your biological parent/child relationship. No matter where your child is, the fact is, he is your child, therefore, the promise of salvation still applies to him.

Sometime ago my friend received a revelation about Paul's and Silas' experience that really brought a new light on Acts 16:31 for me. I realized for the first time that the affliction and suffering of Paul and Silas were also to bring salvation. Through Paul and Silas's persecution, the jailer and his household received salvation. During the time I received this revelation, I was experiencing some difficulties with my daughter. On one occasion, as I was on my knees praying for her, the Lord said, "It is okay that you are interceding on her behalf, but have you considered praying for her acquaintances, those who are being used by Satan to influence her wrongly. Are you praying to destroy the power of darkness over their lives. Do you know I love them and I am concerned about them and desire that they too be saved? They also need prayer." And that struck me like a brick. I was so engrossed in my child, that I forgot that her friends were also heading in the wrong direction and that they too needed prayers. This is something you have to remember, and think about more closely. God has already promised that He will save your children if you can believe. There are children who associate with your child whose parents are not saved. Those children probably have no one praying for them. Many of those children do not have any godly influence in their lives. You need to stand in the gap for those children. They need your prayers. I remember my daughter telling me about one of her friends at school who told her that she never went to church; her parents never took her. They didn't go to church. I don't believe that my daughter met that girl by chance. I believe God allowed that girl to cross paths with my daughter so I would intercede for that family, so He could send someone to witness to that girl about Jesus or so I could be that "someone." There are children like my daughter's friend all around you who need your prayers and your witness.

"And I sought for a man among them, that should make up the hedge and stand in the

gap before me for the land, that I should not destroy it: but I found none."
(Ezekiel 22:30)

You could very well be that one God is looking for to stand in the gap for those children. It could be that God divinely placed those children with your child so you can be that spiritual influence in their lives. God promised you that if you believe on the Lord Jesus Christ, you shall be saved and your household. Some of the parents of your children's friends do not know the Lord Jesus Christ and do not believe on Him. They have no spiritual understanding and cannot teach their children the Word of God nor lead them in the way of God. God sent these children to you so you can pray for them. God may just want you to be that light that will lead these children to Him.

As God revealed this truth to me, I was moved with conviction for being so selfish; and being concerned only about my daughter's salvation. After that, a sense of compassion came over me for my daughter's friends. Jesus reminded me that He died for all children not just mine. I believe that this message is for you also. All children need godly people praying for them.

When I realized how desperately other children needed my prayers, I began to cry out to God, asking him to forgive me for my "selfish" attitude. That night, I made a commitment to the Lord and told Him that I would be an intercessor for my children and for all children. I immediately began crying out to God on behalf of those little ones, praying for their salvation.

I believe that sometimes the Lord allows afflictions to come on His people to bring salvation and deliverance to someone else, as with Paul and Silas.

Our Lord Jesus Christ is a prime example of One who suffered afflictions for the salvation of others. Mom and Dad, your afflictions could very well be to bring about the salvation of others. As you pray for others, God will take care of your children. Going back to Abraham, we find he was a very patient man:

> *"For when God made promises to Abraham, because He could swear by no greater, He swore by Himself,*
> *Saying, surely blessing I will bless thee, and multiplying I will multiply thee. And so after he had patiently endured, he obtained the promise."*   (Hebrews 6:13-15)

The Word of God says, *"after Abraham patiently endured...."* There are two words that described Abraham's character during his period of waiting. They are "patience" and "endurance." He was patient. The definition of patience is endurance. Patience is a characteristic that we all have need of. In this world believers will experience tribulation. But through tribulation, we learn patience. Tribulation teaches you how to be patient.

> *"And not only so, but we glory in tribulation also; knowing that tribulation, worketh patience."*   (Romans 5:3)

Be willing to endure, to wait on the Lord patiently. Although I was praying and interceding for my daughter, I had to wait for His timing. Sometimes I thought the possibility of her giving her life to the Lord was almost impossible; the chances of her coming to the Lord seemed extremely bleak. Each time I saw her going deeper into the way of the world, I could hear God saying, *"be still and know that I am God."*

I remember another occasion after praying, and interceding and fasting for my child and noticing no improvement in her behavior, I began to get tired. Around that time, she and I were setting on the bed, we both picked up different books to read. I was reading the Bible and she was reading a Christian novel I had given her. She was completing a chapter. I had no idea of what was on the page she was reading. I, at the same time unconsciously opened my Bible to Isaiah 40, my eyes immediately focused on verse 31. From what I believe to be the leading of the Lord, I began to read the verse out loud:

> *"But they that wait upon the Lord shall renew their strength; they shall mount up with wings as eagles; they shall run and not be weary; and they shall walk, and not faint."*

As I was reading the verse, my daughter interrupted, and said, "Mamie!" From the tone of her voice, I thought something had happened. I said, "Is something wrong?" She said, "that's the same verse I am reading in this book." I thought she was joking, but when I looked on the page she was reading, it was the exact same verse. We both knew that the Lord was telling us something.

You may think this was a coincidence, but I don't think so. I don't think anything happens in the life of a believer by chance. I believe God divinely orders His children's footsteps. Psalms 37:23 says, *"The steps of a good man are ordered by the Lord: and He delights in his way."* He knew how I felt about my daughter's wrong behavior. He knew I was on the verge of giving up. So He encouraged my heart with His word to give me the strength I needed to continue to wait.

His Word assured me that if I waited on Him, in His time, I would see a change in her life. I know without a doubt this was His doing. The Bible says, *"In the mouth of two or three witnesses shall every Word be established."* (II Corinthians 13:1) So with my daughter reading the same verse I was reading, God established His Word that my waiting would pay off. That was a special moment for me.

Because of those assuring words from the Lord, I was able to continue in prayer and fasting for her.

Around this same time, my daughter came to me and said, "Mamie, how come I just can't have a normal lifestyle. I mean just having a normal lifestyle, doing what I want to do, like those other kids? Their parents let them do things that I can't do."

You see, there were some things other kids parents let them do that I didn't allow her to do. For example, certain movies and TV shows she was not allowed to watch that other parents had no problem allowing their children to watch. She couldn't use certain words that some of her friends used. I didn't allow her to go to certain places her friends were allowed to go. I would tell her that I was not doing this to keep her from having fun. I loved her and wanted her to have fun but that there were just certain things we did not permit in our home. As Christians, certain things were not right for us and we had rules and standards she had to abide by. She would say, "Mamie, some kids do wrong things all the time and get away with it. They never get caught or get in trouble, but every time I try to do the same things, it never works for me, I end up getting in trouble. Why? Mamie, I just don't understand."

I would tell her, "Because I am praying for you, God is protecting you, He doesn't want you being destroyed. Too many people are praying for you, He will not allow Satan to destroy you. You may think that other children are getting away with wrong doings, but sooner or later those children will get caught. The Bible says, *"...be sure your sins will find you out."* (Numbers 32:23) No one gets away with doing wrong. In God's time, He exposes all wrongdoers. God loves those children and He also desires that they come to know him. We are to pray for your friends."

One evening, after a confrontation with my daughter, I began to cry out to God saying, "Lord, when? When will she surrender her life to you?"

In that same, ever familiar, still small voice, the Lord whispered to my heart as usual, "Be still and know that I am God." That same evening, my daughter called me and said, "Mamie, I want to talk." So we went for a car ride.

She told me, "Mamie, I don't feel good in my body, pray for me." I reached over and took her by the hand and began to pray for her. That night I asked her if she was ready to give her life to the Lord. She said, "Yes!" I felt her sincerity.

That night, she invited Christ into her heart. I am truly grateful to God for that. That night she made the greatest commitment of her life. You may say, "That's great, her trouble is over."

Remember, there is still that war between the flesh and the spirit. Satan never stop his work because a person receives Christ as their Lord and Savior. This is the time he even tries harder to cause that person to fall. But no matter what Satan's plans are, God's plans supersedes his. God is gradually maturing her. As Jesus said in Mark 4:28, "For the earth bringeth forth fruit of herself, first the blade, then the ear, after that the full corn in the ear." This is how I see God working in her life.

I see spiritual growth. She is not where she ought to be yet, but I can say that she is not where she used to be. I see improvement. And I am grateful to God for what He is doing with her. I have peace that God is in control of my daughter's life.

My prayer is that she will continue to grow in the Lord and accomplish all that God has for her to do in her lifetime. I know without a doubt that Christ will complete the work He has already begun in Her.

"Being confident of this very thing, that He which hath begun a good work in her will perform it until the day of Jesus Christ."
(Philippians 1:6)

"And let us not be weary in well doing; for in due season we shall reap, if we faint not." (Galatians 6:9)

Parents, please do not give up on your perseverance in prayers, fasting, and loving your child. God is faithful. Your labor is not in vain. Be encouraged and know that God is true to His promises. Every effort you make, whether in prayer, fasting or intercession, God will remain faithful. After you have done all you can, then wait and see God move in the life of your child.

Never, Never Give Up, THERE IS HOPE!

Additional books are available at your local bookstore, or from the publisher. For further information, or speaking engagements, you may also contact the Author by writing to her at the following address:

Elizabeth W. Brown
P.O. Box 200482,
Shaker Heights, Ohio   44120

FOR ADDITIONAL COPIES WRITE:

Impac *Chris* *ian*
Books

332 Leffingwell Ave., Suite 101
Kirkwood, MO 63122

AVAILABLE AT YOUR LOCAL BOOKSTORE, OR YOU MAY
ORDER DIRECTLY. Toll-Free, order-line only M/C, DISC,
or VISA 1-800-451-2708.